My Friend John

Also by Graham Old

Fiction

The Asylum Diaries

The Removal

Pete, the Poet

Sold his Soul

Nonfiction

Mastering the Leisure Induction

Revisiting Hypnosis

The Elman Induction

The Hypnotic Handshakes

The Anxiety Guide

Therapeutic Inductions

My Friend

John

by Graham Old

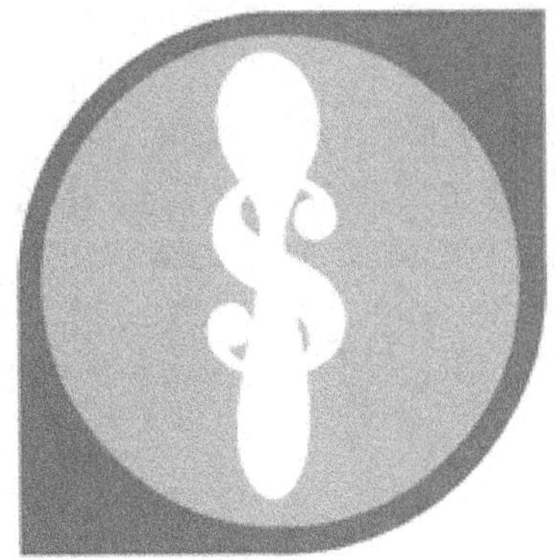

My Friend John

Copyright © GRAHAM OLD

First published 2018 by Plastic Spoon

www.plasticspoon.info

Preface

My Friend John is the fifth book in our *Inductions Masterclass* series.

Our aim for each book in the series has been that they will act as useful introductions to the wider workings of hypnosis by extracting valuable insights from the practice of specific inductions. This book is no different.

So, whilst we present My Friend John and share details to assist with its delivery, we will also be simultaneously presenting ideas and practices that are helpful for the wider use of hypnosis.

It continues to be a matter of some surprise that few books take a similar course of action. When the time comes that someone else copies this format, or at the very least mirrors the intention, we would consider it a compliment. As it is, it remains the case that not only are there very few books which use an induction to teach wider lessons, there are actually very few works which focus on and unpack an individual induction in any real depth.

As with the other books in the series, we are again aiming to duplicate the level, detail and quality of information you might receive at a live training. So, we aim to provide in-depth practical information, point to useful theoretical discussions, anticipate questions from 'the Floor' and handle natural diversions and meandering discussions.

Other books in this series have focused on topics such as Observation, Utilisation, Fractionation and Anchoring. The current work looks at the technique of insertive eye-contact, the theory of rolling with resistance, finding your trance voice and the notion of embedded ideas. As with all of our products and training, our aim here is to point to deep theory through sharing practical knowledge in a refreshingly clear and accessible way.

Acknowledgements

It appears to be the case that I am incapable of writing a hypnosis book without acknowledging the influence of Stephen Brooks. However, this is not necessarily a bad thing. If all my own writing does is point people to the man who personifies hypnosis with a heart, it will be a worthy achievement.

All Rights Reserved

Disclaimer

This book is not meant as a replacement for proper training in hypnosis or psychotherapy.

These ideas are offered as a way to enhance your current skills, with a view to more effectively understanding hypnosis and helping others. Please be aware that any experimentation with the ideas presented in this book is undertaken at your own risk and responsibility.

At all times when practising hypnosis, it is your

responsibility to ensure that you comply with the laws, regulations and codes of your home country, region, state or territory.

Contents

Introduction

The *My Friend John* technique, developed by Milton Erickson, is a much-admired, but rarely-employed induction. It has a certain reputation for difficulty, which this hypnotist believes does not match the execution of the technique.

In fact, as *My Friend John* can be viewed as a covert induction, there is an assumption that it can only be carried out by the most skilled master hypnotists. In contrast, we will present a model of *My Friend John* in this book that can be employed by beginners as well as experts. We will even teach a variation that can be completely overt.

The various versions of *My Friend John* that we will describe all share a common core. They are framed as a description of someone else being lead into hypnosis. That is as far as an induction needs to go before earning the right to be labelled *My Friend John*. Some discuss a previous client who was hypnotised. Some ask the current client to imagine that there is someone there who is being hypnotised in front of them. Some involve actually hypnotising someone, whilst the client observes. This book will cover all these variations and some others besides.

As with the other books in this series, we will provide a number of transcripts of the induction in action.

However, this book contains more than the usual number of transcripts, as it demonstrates the various ways that the induction can be utilised.

Along with the transcripts, this book demonstrates a number of the principles at work in the induction. It makes these principles explicit and shares them as useful for the wider practice of hypnosis and NLP. The induction is therefore presented as a microcosm of the wider field of hypnosis and hypnotherapy.

The book ends with a trouble-shooting section and Frequently Asked Questions. Our intention is that readers will feel as prepared as they do informed and quickly find themselves in a position to confidently use and enjoy the *My Friend John* Induction.

There are numerous exercises to be completed throughout the book, to practically reinforce the information presented within. These are presented as an essential element of the book, not an optional extra. It is suggested that you take part in these with what teachers of Zen call a 'Beginner's Mind' – humbly enjoying the experience of learning and experiencing something new.

Terminology used

Throughout this book you may find us referring to 'trance' and at times using terminology such as 'subconscious', deepening, being 'under' hypnosis and so on. Please bear in mind that these are phenomenological descriptions, merely meant to convey what the hypnotee may be experiencing. We are not endorsing any particular interpretation of hypnosis, or taking sides in the perennial debates over the nature of trance or the existence of a special hypnotic state.

For more on our experiential model of hypnosis, which fits comfortably with all the major schools of Hypnosis, see our book, '*Therapeutic Inductions*.'

EXERCISE

Describe to someone else how you typically like to lead a person into hypnosis.

Share as much detail as is necessary for them to be able to picture and/or imagine the hypnosis taking place.

Why Learn My Friend John?

If I can begin with a confession, *My Friend John* is one of my favourite inductions. Therefore, it is slightly difficult for me to remain objective about it. Why learn it? Why *not*?! However, I will do my best to present some of the positive benefits that can be obtained from including *My Friend John* in your current arsenal of inductions, aside from my particular preferences.

Comfortably Covert

In some of its manifestations, *My Friend John* can be considered a covert induction. All appearances suggest that it is merely a discussion about someone else being hypnotised. Yet, along the way, the engaged listener is drawn into trance themselves.

My Friend John is a useful starting point for anyone wanting to develop their skills in covert or conversational hypnosis. If all else fails, you have simply had an interesting discussion about someone going in to hypnosis. At that point, you could continue with any other induction and find that things will run smoothly, as you have already seeded a number of significant ideas.

Alternatively, if the conversational element of the induction does not achieve the desired ends, it is perfectly straightforward to turn things around, become overt and ask your client to now take the place of your previously imagined friend named John.

> Hypnotist: "Now that we've described that, giving you some idea of my part in the process, as well as some clues as to what it can look like and how it is experienced, I wonder if I can invite you to become *My Friend John* and prepare to go in to hypnosis?"

To the unsuspecting observer, nothing you have done has failed. You have merely described what is going to happen, by using someone else's experience as an example.

This makes *My Friend John* the perfect induction to use whilst you are honing your conversational hypnosis skills.

Painless Practice

For all of the reasons discussed above, *My Friend John* is a perfect induction to practice. It is completely risk-free, with a number of possible positive outcomes.

It can be practised conversationally or overtly. It can even be partially practised, as how far along you go with the process is completely up to you. You may keep going until you see if you can achieve hypnotic phenomena, or you may simply be satisfied with causing changes in someone's breathing and inducing relaxation.

Variety of Versions

One of the things that I particularly value about *My Friend John* is the number of different variations. This sometimes surprises new hypnotists, who have perhaps only been taught one version of the induction and presumed that was the "correct" version.

In reality, it is more appropriate to think of *My Friend John* as being a family of inductions, all united under a common theme. That theme can be expressed in a whole manner of different ways. This book contains more transcripts than others in the series precisely because we are aiming to demonstrate the number of ways that *My Friend John* can be employed.

Subtle Springboard

As suggested above, *My Friend John* is perfect for diverting into other inductions or approaches. It can be used as a pre-talk for a different induction, or as the first part of an induction. It can be used to transition from an indirect to a direct approach. It can even be utilised as a seamless way to move from your intake, to your more formal hypnotic work.

It would be appropriate to think of *My Friend John* as a multi-purpose tool that is about as reliable as any induction can be.

EXERCISE

Describe to someone how you typically like to lead someone into hypnosis, this time focusing on the description of what the hypnotee is likely to be feeling as you do so.

Initial Transcript

The following transcript is a real-life example of the *My Friend John* induction in action. The client was an 18-year old dad who had been referred by Social Services for support with 'anger management.' They were not necessarily resistant to being helped, though there was some clear hostility towards the Social Worker, which was naturally initially projected onto the hypnotist as well.

H(ypnotist): "I'm going to ask you to do something that, at first, might seem a little bit strange."

C(lient): "Right."

H: "But it's easy. And some people even enjoy it."

C: "Okay."

H: "And all I am going to ask you to do is… look at that chair there…" [points to an empty chair on the other side of the room] "…and imagine that there is someone sat there that I am hypnotising."

C: "Is that it?"

H: "That's it."

C: "Okay."

H: "Great, so this person, I'll call them John, is sat there..." [Client shuffles slightly in their seat] "...just relaxing, getting comfortable... and I tell them, '*any time you want to get even more comfortable, you can move around in your chair.*'"

[At times, the Hypnotist's voice changes slightly, in tone and tempo, when they are directly addressing "John." The same slight change can be seen in the transcript in the use of *italics*.]

H: "And you can..." [timed to coincide with the client's next inhalation] "...*take a nice deep breath... that's it. And then you can just... let it out again.*"

"And I say to them, 'What I would like you to do now is just *rest your eyes* at a spot on the wall in front of you. And, sometimes, your focus will drift slightly and when that happens you can just *gently redirect your focus back to that spot on the wall that you're looking at now.*'

"Your eyes may grow tired and that is fine. Just keep them open for as long as you would like to… And *you may notice a narrowing of your focus, a kind of tunnel-vision…* that's perfectly natural and just serves to remind you to *keep your eyes resting over there."*

[The hypnotist turns to face the client and speaks quietly, almost as if they don't want "John" to hear.]

H: "Of course, as you're watching John…" [assuming compliance and hallucination] "…you can notice as he responds and begins to *slip into trance."*

C: "Yeah."

H: "So, John, *continue to breathe in that nice and easy way…"* [turns to face client, as if to check they are still there, then turns back to John] "…almost as if you are continuing to *breathe-in peace and calm…* and *let go of any stress and tension."*

"And as you continue to relax in that way, you can *let all of your facial muscles relax* nice and gently… That's it. *Relaxing from the top of your head. Tension leaving your forehead and your temples. The tiny muscles around your eyes relaxing…"* [timed to coincide with the client's next blink] "…*that's right* …your facial muscles relaxing and flattening…"

"Some people are surprised by how easy it is to *go into trance."* [Turns to client and nods and then says...] "...And John shows us how easy and natural that can be..."

"The *muscles in your neck relaxing*, such that you might *feel more comfortable* if your head gently drops forward or back, or simply *rest where you are*, as you continue to *breathe in and out nice and easy*..."

"...your *shoulders relaxing now...* [notices client's shoulders droop slightly...] "...that's it ...getting *comfortable in that seat... relaxation coming naturally*..."

"...And as you continue to *relax further and further*, drifting *deeper and deeper into that experience*, allowing that to spread and enjoying the realisation that *you had this ability all along*, to *relax deeply and rapidly in your own way*..."

"...And with some clients I might encourage them to *carry on relaxing*, as I count down from 10 to 1... and we sometimes have people imagine themselves at the top of a staircase, with ten steps, each step down doubling their current level of relaxation... So I would count..." [timed to coincide with the client's next exhalation] "... 10 ...doubling that relaxation... 9 ...deeper and deeper... 8 ...relaxing even more..."

[Still facing John, as if speaking to them.]

"But I know that with you, you are such a natural at this, and you relax so easily and *let yourself go*, that I don't need to do anything like ask you to *imagine a staircase*. Or count down for you. It's almost as if *every time you breathe out*, you *relax twice as deeply*, almost as if you were beginning to *walk down those stairs*, without me even needing to count for you... Just finding that every breath is like another step down, another step into relaxation... as that continues to spread throughout your body."

[The client's eyes appear heavy and their head drops occasionally.]

H: "And any time you want to allow that head to rest, eyes gently closed, you can *let your head gently drop forward...* going deeper and deeper into that experience... as it continues to *spread from the top of your head all the way down* to the tip of your toes...

[The client's eyes begin to blink rapidly.]

"*...And you can let those eyes close whenever you like...* letting go... *resting comfortably now...*"

[The client's eyes continue to blink rapidly.]

"...sinking, drifting, floating, *deeper into that experience...* And it may even seem like those eyes have a mind of their own. So any time you feel that *they want to close*, you can go ahead and *let them*."

[The client's eyes close.]

"...letting go... and thoroughly enjoying the process as you do so..."

25

EXERCISE

Practice the *My Friend John* induction with someone.

Preface it by being up-front about the fact that you want to try a new way of leading someone into hypnosis.

Retrospective Commentary

The transcript which we have just looked at was not a script that was followed. It was a transcript of an impromptu induction. *My Friend John* was chosen because of the client's potential "resistance."[1] Nothing else about the induction was planned in advance.

Therefore, the commentary that follows is not a description of why things were planned the way that they were. Neither is it, in all honesty, a discussion of why certain decisions were taken when they were. Anyone who has worked in such a manner will be able to confirm that most decisions are made intuitively in situations such as that captured in the transcript. Instead, this commentary is a discussion of what happened, with no claims to planning, intention or therapeutic genius. Sometimes, when you are working in the flow, you just get lucky.

The Set-Up

As stated before the transcript, this client was projecting a small amount of hostility towards the hypnotist. It was assumed that this was an extension of

---

1   In future chapters, it will become clear why the word *resistance* is in speech marks.

his displeasure at his treatment at the hands of Social Services. However, there was no direct hostility and the client had been given the responsibility of choosing his own therapist and even the model of therapy. In that sense, he was choosing to be in my office, to some degree.

There is no reason given to the client as to why they are asked to witness the induction of an invisible hypnotee. If there had been a more palpable level of resistance, I may have proceeded by saying that I was asking the client to help me out with an experiment. It is not usually necessary to say how or why watching me carry out an invisible induction is a useful experiment, but it is almost always enough to provoke a curious engagement with the process.

In this case, the wording used was:

> H(ypnotist): "I'm going to ask you to do something that, at first, might seem a little bit strange."

Being up-front about how "strange" your request is going to sound is a disarmingly simple way to help people put their defences down. They are expecting you to say something unusual and may even consider themselves challenged to be one of those who can accept it.

Witnessing a Current Hypnotee

In this case, I was not describing a previous induction I had performed on someone. I was instead taking my client through the induction that I might use if there were someone else in the room that I was hypnotising. This has an impact on the present-tense language of the induction.

I was able to give direct suggestions to my client, cloaked as suggestions to John, precisely because I was describing someone that I was apparently hypnotising on the other side of the room.

A glaring example of this can be seen in retrospect:

> "What I would like you to do now is just *rest your eyes* at a spot on the wall in front of you. And, sometimes, your focus will drift slightly and when that happens you can just gently redirect your focus back on that spot on the wall that you're looking at now.

> "Your eyes may grow tired and that is fine. Just keep them open for as long as you would like to... And you may notice a narrowing of your focus, a kind of tunnel-vision... that's perfectly natural and just serves to remind you to *keep your eyes resting over there*.

Eye-fixation

The kind of induction that is described as happening is an eye-fixation. This is an ideal choice because it perfectly mirrors the experience of the client. That means that my suggestions to John are immediately applicable to the client.

However, other inductions can be used. Any induction that relies on physical relaxation is useful, as you can generally assume that as you describe this being achieved by John, it is experienced by your client. Guided visualisations and similar inductions can work well, as your client is able to go inside to imagine what it is that John is imagining.

You can even utilise more rapid inductions. The easiest way to do this is by having the client act out what you did with John. Alternatively, you might ask them to close their eyes and imagine what you describe. However, the key here is in providing the client with an experience which will rapidly change their state. It is more than possible in a *My Friend John* scenario, but may take some priming, not to mention practice.

Embedded Commands

You will have noticed the rather blatant use of what some people call "embedded commands":

[The client's eyes appear heavy and their head drops occasionally.]

H: "And any time you want to allow that head to rest, eyes gently closed, you can *let you head gently drop forward...* going deeper and deeper into that experience... as it continues to spread from the top of your head all the way down to the tip of your toes...

[The client's eyes begin to blink rapidly.]

"*...And you can let those eyes close whenever you like...* letting go... *resting comfortably* *now..."*

It is possible to be so blatant precisely because this is the expected behaviour if I was hypnotising someone in the other chair. On one occasion, I give a justification for turning round and firing an embedded command directly at the client:

> "Your eyes may grow tired and that is fine. Just keep them open for as long as you would like to... And you may notice a narrowing of your focus, a kind of tunnel-vision... that's perfectly natural and just serves to remind you to *keep your eyes resting over there.*"

> [The hypnotist turns to face the client and speaks quietly, almost as if they don't want "John" to hear.]

> "Of course, as you're watching John..." [assuming compliance and hallucination] "...you can notice as he responds and begins to *slip into trance.*"

Although I am looking at and speaking directly to my client, I use the excuse of talking to them about John as a cover. Nothing about the process feels manipulative or controlling, as it is all taking place within the context of an induction into hypnosis.

The End Game

Speaking of being manipulative, hypnotists who begin

to use *My Friend John* sometimes worry that it will feel coercive or deceitful to clients. I have not found this to be the case.

It is certainly true that some clients will notice what you are doing and will perhaps even point it out to you. One or two clients will gladly tell you afterwards that they knew what you were doing, to make it clear that you did not manage to get anything passed them. Yet, it is rare for them to object or protest. After all, unless you are proceeding completely without their permission (and if you are creative, even covert hypnosis can be done ethically with permission), your client is there to be hypnotised. For them to complain that you were doing precisely that would be unusual.

The outcome that is more common is that a client will realise what is happening part of the way through the induction. However, by the time they are at that point, they are in such a pleasant state of mind that they are more than happy to continue being guided by you.

The Deepener

We will later spend a chapter discussing various ways to deepen this induction. In this case, I introduced the notion of a relaxing staircase, but then allowed the client to direct themselves down it, in time with their breathing.

Termination

It may not be obvious when to stop the pretence of hypnotising someone else. In this example, eye-closure was the termination point. However, other transcripts in this book will demonstrate that the induction kept going until other hypnotic phenomena had been achieved, even if that is simply eye catalepsy.

The important point is that you want to reach a place where you are confident that the client is now responding directly to your suggestions. When that occurs, there is no longer any need for John. You may even choose to make this transition explicit by using your client's name at that point.

EXERCISE

Practice the *My Friend John* induction on someone. Your aim at this stage is to simply get used to the process, so do not get too hung up on how far 'under' your practice partner goes.

Become familiar with using a slightly different voice when you are speaking to John.

Describing Earlier Hypnosis

It is possible to carry out this induction by describing to someone how you previously hypnotised someone else. Therefore, at times you would be speaking in the past tense, unless you are directly quoting something you said to "John."

The version that follows is useful when working with children and rather than *My Friend John* it is perhaps more accurate to label it, *Your Best Friend*. This version can be used in the present tense (i.e. "imagine that I am hypnotising your best friend..."). However, I find it useful to employ the past tense, even if to a limited degree, to reassure the child that their friend experienced it all and it was fine.

H(ypnotist): "I'm going to ask you to use your imagination for me. Are you good at pretending?."

C(lient): "Yeah."

H: "Excellent. This will be easy for you then. And what I want to ask you to pretend is that your best friend was sat in that chair just a few minutes ago, just before you."

C: [Laughs]

H: "What's your best friend's name?"

C: "Lacey."

H: "Lacey. Okay. So, do you think you can do that? Just imagine that Lacey came to see me earlier and she was sat in that chair."

C: "Okay."

H: "Great. And I am going to describe for you, everything that I did with Lacey, so you can see what we do here and how much fun it is. How does that sound?"

C: "Good."

H: "Good! It *is* good, you're right! Now, I will just say that what you do whilst I'm describing what I did with Lacey is completely up to you. You can sit there and imagine watching Lacey. Or you can imagine that you are Lacey. You can even imagine that you are me, telling her what to do! That's all up to you. Okay?"

C: "Yeah."

H: "Great. Let's get started then. I am now going to act out everything that I did with Lacey to show you what happened earlier on. So… [turns to face the empty chair] Thank you for coming in, Lacey. It is lovely to meet you."

C: [Laughs]

H: "Then I said, 'And the very first thing you can do is just get as comfortable as possible.' [Turns to face the client and smiles. They smile back and shift slightly in their chair. Hypnotist turns to Lacey.] 'That's right, *just get nice and comfortable.'*"

H: [Turns to client.] "Imagine what she would have looked like when she was nice and comfortable."

H: [Turns back to face the empty chair] "And I want you to imagine that you're somewhere where you are nice and relaxed, where you can just be you and completely chill out. It could be lying on a beach, snoozing on the sofa, playing in the park. Anywhere that you can relax and feel good." [Turns to client and asks where she thinks Lacey would choose.]

C: "I think she'd choose the beach."

H: "She *did* choose the beach! Good guess! [Smiles and turns back to Lacey.] And I would like you to imagine that you are at the beach and you are perfectly safe and completely comfortable. And you lay down in the sand to enjoy the Sun."

C: [Breaths out.]

H: "That's it. Letting go of all stress and tension. And as you breathe-in [waits for client to inhale], taking in peace and calm. And in fact, every breath you take can help you to relax deeper and deeper, as you *just enjoy that experience* of imagining you are on the beach.

H: [Turns to face Client] "Notice how their breathing has slowed down and become nice and steady, as they relax further and further."

H: [Turns back to Lacey] "Then I said, 'And I wonder if you can imagine feeling the warmth of the Sun on the top of your head. Nice and warm and cozy and relaxing. And maybe you can *imagine the warmth beginning to move down your body*, from the top of your head, over your eyes and slowly all the way down to your feet, *relaxing each part that it passes over*, until your whole body *feel nice and warm and cosy and relaxed*... from the top of your head to the tips of your toes.'"

C: [Closes their eyes.]

H: "And I would like you to imagine that your eyes are so relaxed that they just won't open. They're just too tired and comfortable. You know that feeling when someone is trying to wake you up to get ready for school and your eyes are still asleep, just too tired to open. I want you to enjoy that same feeling of relaxed tiredness in your eyes. And when you've got that feeling in your eyes, hold onto it and don't let go. And I want you to try and open your eyes and I want you to discover that they are just too relaxed to open. Just pretend that they are far too happy being closed and comfortable. And when you've got that feeling, go ahead and try and open them and find that as long as you hold onto that relaxation they just stay shut."

H: [Looks over to Client, whose eyes are closed. She is raising her eyebrows, apparently trying to open her eyes.]

H: "That's perfect. And now you can stop trying and just *let go and let them relax*. And you can allow that whole feeling of relaxation to spread as it passes down your body once again. Letting go, nice and warm and comfortable and relaxed.

"And, again, every breath that you take can increase this experience for you, feeling even better with every breath.

"And in a moment, Sophie, one of your arms is going to feel incredibly light, as if it is too light to hold down. I don't know if it will be your left hand or your right hand, but one of your hands will begin to feel incredibly light. [Notices a finger twitch in the client's left hand.] That's right."

H: [Begins to speak on the client's inhalations...] "And it might start in the fingertips, or it might start at the wrist, but very slowly that arm is going to begin rising up. In its own time, it will feel so light that it just starts to rise up into the air, as if it has one of those helium balloons tied onto it, and your arm floats up with the balloon.

C: [Left arms begins to gently rise up, moving from side to side as it does so.]

H: [Still speaking on the inhalations.] "Swaying in the wind, like that balloon, rising higher and higher.

"And as that hand continues to float up in that light and floaty way, when the hand touches your face you can go into a very deep sleep. And sleep when you're in hypnosis is like a lovely deep day-dream. A part of you can still hear everything that I say to you, but your conscious mind is off playing waaaay over there, whilst I speak to your unconscious here. [Hand touches face.] And you can just feel so comfortably relaxed that you just continue to sink deeper and deeper down into that wonderful feeling."

EXERCISE

Practice *My Friend John*.

Get valuable feedback from your practice partner.

At what points did they feel themselves responding to the suggestions given to John?

Were there any points when they felt held back or dissociated from John's experience?

GRAHAM OLD

42

Some Observations

It is fitting that this chapter is called 'Some Observations' as we reflect on the transcript we have just seen. The very first thing to draw out of it is the level of observation taking place by the hypnotist.

Elsewhere, we have spoken of observation as one of the core skills employed by the effective hypnotist.[2] We went so far as to quote Sigmund Freud on the matter, who wrote, 'Suspend judgement and give impartial attention to everything there is to observe.'[3]

Although it may appear as if the hypnotist is focused on "Lacey," they are actually intimately aware of every response that their client makes. This includes their level of breathing, shifting in the chair, eye-closure and so on. This is absolutely necessary if the hypnotist is to be aware of how far the client is engaging with the process. There is no point in the hypnotist rushing ahead to phenomena, if the client is still purely imagining that everything is happening to Lacey and not personally involved, engaged or responding at all.

You will want to pay attention to things like the level

---

2   Old, G. (2014). *Mastering the Leisure Induction*. Milton Keynes: Plastic Spoon.

3   Freud, S. (1909). Analysis of a phobia in a five-year old boy. *Standard Edition*, 10, 3-152. London: Hogarth Press, 1955.

of colour in their cheeks, rate of breathing, flattening of the facial muscles, changes in the rate of blinking and so on. In effect, you are looking for any change that can most reliably be explained as a response to the words being spoken to Lacey or John.

It may well be that you become aware of these changes a long time before your client does. In that case, you can feed them back. So, in the example just seen, we have the following:

> "And in a moment, one of your arms is going to feel incredibly light, as if it is too light to hold down. I don't know if it will be your left hand or your right hand, but one of your hands will begin to feel incredibly light. [Notices a finger twitch in the client's left hand.] That's right."

> H: [Begins to speak on the client's inhalations...] "And it might start in the fingertips, or it might start at the wrist, but very slowly that arm is going to begin rising up. In its own time, it will feel so light that it just starts to rise up into the air, as if it has one of those helium balloons tied onto it, and your arm floats up with the balloon.

> C: [Left arms begins to gently rise up, moving from side to side as it does so.]

> H: [Still speaking on the inhalations.] "Swaying in the wind, like that balloon, rising higher and higher.

The "that's right," the mention of the fingertips and the allusion to 'swaying in the wind,' are all responses to what had been observed of the client's behaviour.

Whether or not the client is aware of what is happening to them – i.e. not just Lacey – by then is not the point. Their experience will provide you with clues as to how to pace what is taking place and then lead them further into the experience.

You may have noticed that although we were discussing a previous hypnotic experience, the repetition of the earlier instructions provides the hypnotist with present-tense commands. These are useful to pass on to the client, as they enable you to be more direct under the pretence of repeating what took place previously. However, they are couched within a past-tense context, which serves to reassure the young client.

EXERCISE

Practice *My Friend John*, aiming for eye-closure in your practice partner.

Do not be afraid to give permission for them to go in to hypnosis, if you feel that they are getting close, but holding back for some reason.

Collect any valuable feedback they may have to give you at the end.

Passively Witnessing Hypnosis

In the previous example, the client was given the option to imagine they were the hypnotist, or the client, or both. It is not necessary to give them such explicit options, as they will tend to gradually switch from associating with the hypnotist to associating with the client as the process progresses.

The following transcript is an example of a time when the client was invited to merely witness what took place as "John" was hypnotised.

> H(ypnotist): "We're going to do something a little bit different now. I would like you to imagine that I am hypnotising someone else in that chair there. And you can imagine whoever you like. I think of *My Friend John*, you might think of a friend of yours, or a family member, or even your unconscious, whilst your conscious mind stays in this seat here. Does that make sense?"
>
> C(lient): "So, I'm imagining you hypnotising them?"
>
> H: "Yep. It's as simple as that. I will go through the steps of hypnotising the person in that chair and you can just imagine and notice

what happens."

C: "Okay."

H: "Great. So the first thing I would do is invite them to get comfortable. So, [turning to the empty chair] you can just get comfortable in that chair. And if you need to move around at any point to get even more comfortable, that's perfectly fine."

H: [Turning back to the client] "And you can notice as they get themselves nice and comfortable in that chair."

H: [Turning to the empty chair] "And now [wait for the client's next inhalation] take a nice deep breath and then [wait for exhalation] just let it out. Again, another deep breath in... and then let it out. And you can keep breathing in this way, relaxing more and more as you do so, as if you breathe in peace and calm and let out any stress and tension."

H: [Turning back to the client] "And you can notice as they relax in time with their breathing."

H: [Turning to the empty chair] "And as that relaxation spreads with every breath, you can allow that feeling to increase as it moves through every inch of your body. Every breath you take and every word that I say allows you to go deeper and deeper into that experience."

H: [Turning back to the client] "And just notice as they become more and more relaxed."

H: [Turning to the empty chair] "Just allowing that relaxation to work its way from the top of your head, all the way down your body. And as that relaxation spreads, you can notice the tendency for your eyes to want to close. Each time you blink, it might be as if it becomes harder for you to open your eyes, as they are just so relaxed they want to stay closed."

C: [Eyes blink more slowly]

H: "And you don't have to fight that, though you can keep your eyes open as long as you want to. And any time you feel the tendency for your eyes to want to stay closed, just notice it and notice what that feels like."

H: [Turning back to the client] "And you can notice anything that happens that tells you they are ready to go into hypnosis. [Speaking on the client's exhalations] Maybe changes in their breathing. Maybe their blinking becomes slower, or their eyelids flutter. Just notice whatever you notice.

C: [Blinks very slowly and appears to struggle to open eyes afterwards.]

H: "That's right. [Turning back to the empty

chair] And whenever you are ready, when you know that your eyes would be more relaxed if you allowed them to stay shut, [turning slightly to the client, as if just checking they are still watching...] you can close your eyes and let go. [Turns back to empty chair] As you relax deeper and deeper and those eyes want to stay shut now, you can just let go and go inside, entering that nice day-dreamy state."

H: [Turning back to the client, whose eyes are on the verge of closing...] "That's right. And you can go inside with them, Terry, allowing yourself to enjoy that experience. [Client's eyes close and their head drops slightly forward.] All the way..."

EXERCISE

Practice the Passively Witnessing Hypnosis version of *My Friend John*.

Deepening My Friend John

Deepening with the *My Friend John* induction is an incredibly straightforward procedure. More often than not, the point where you would usually move from the induction to the deepener is where you shift from addressing "John," to addressing the client directly.

Your client will notice the shift, even if their eyes are closed and the only difference is your tone of voice. This in itself has a deepening effect.

Alternatively, you might choose to use the transition from induction to deepener to begin switching from John to your client and back again. This gives the impression that something is happening and creates an experience of being drawn in to what is taking place. Then, to complete the deepener, you begin addressing the client directly.

Another way to deepen with *My Friend John* is seen in the first transcript in this book. Essentially, you describe what you would do with John or anyone else and then say that it is not necessary in this case. However, as you have described it, the client has begun to experience it for themselves.

As the deepening in *My Friend John* takes place at a natural point in the process, it is to be expected that any number of popular deepeners will do the trick. A number are shared below.

Staircase Deepener

The staircase deepener is a common choice with hypnotists. If the hypnosis is described as – or accompanied by – relaxation, this deepener is a natural one to employ. It is particularly effective if moving down the steps is tied-in with the client's breathing.

> "Sitting there, comfortable and relaxed, you can become aware of a staircase. Visualise, imagine or pretend that you are at the top of a beautiful staircase, with a grand, ornate banister running alongside it.
>
> "And you can notice that there are ten steps leading gently down. And these ten steps will lead you even deeper into that relaxation you are enjoying. So, in a moment I am going to begin counting from 10 down to 1 and you can move down a step with each number that I count off. And what you will find is that each step takes you down deeper into relaxation. And the deeper down you go, the more comfortable and the more relaxed you will become.
>
> "So, we start now at 10, deeply relaxed and comfortable."
>
> [Each number is called out as the client exhales.]
>
> "9 – moving deeper down, deeper into that relaxation.

8 – doubling that relaxation with every step, doubling that comfort.

7 – more and more relaxed.

6 – deeper and deeper.

5 – more and more and more relaxed; half way there now.

4 – doubling that experience with every step.

3 – more and more and more relaxed

2 – deeper and deeper into that comfort and relaxation.

1 – all the way down, deep down into that comfortable state of relaxation, all the way down..."

A common strategy once the client has reached the bottom of the staircase is to have them then walk through a doorway into a special room, or special place outside where they can visualise and access resources.

Find a Lower Level

A straightforward means of intensifying your client's experience is to have their subconscious find a deeper level. You may not be comfortable with the language of 'subconscious' or 'deepening' if that does not sit well with your model of hypnosis. However, any language can be employed to assist your client in maintaining and magnifying their current experience. All the language we use at such times is metaphorical any way.

> "And your subconscious mind knows that you are able to take even more from this experience. So, I am going to count from 3 to 1 and as I do so, I will take hold of your arm like so [lifts up arm briefly by the wrist]. Then when I reach 1 I will drop your hand into your lap and that will be a signal for your subconscious to take you even deeper into this experience.

> "So, 3 [lifts up arm a few inches]... 2... 1 [drops arm into their lap]... and deeper down.

> "And we will do that one more time. And this time, your subconscious mind will take you deeper to precisely the level of trance that you need to be at to complete the work that we are going to do together.

> "So, 3 [lifts up arm a few inches]... 2... 1 [drops arm into their lap]... and all the way down."

In that example, I have intentionally mixed-up the type of language used to show the flexibility that can be employed. The most important thing is that you are using language that is meaningful to your client. The second most important is that you are congruent in what you are saying.

Continue to Deepen naturally

Perhaps the simplest way to deepen with *My Friend John* is to do so naturally. Obvious examples would be:

> "And any sounds that you hear will only serve to remind you what a natural process this is, allowing you to sink deeper into that experience."

Or:

> "And as you let that breath out, you can relax and feel great. And the better you feel, the deeper you'll go. And the deeper you go, the better you feel."

Or:

> "And every breath that you take, and every word that I say will cause you to go deeper and deeper into that state."

EXERCISE

Practice *My Friend John* with a deepener.

Does any particular deepener feel more appropriate, given the induction?

Direct Hypnosis

It is possible to perform the *My Friend John* induction without reference to another person in the room. Instead, you simply describe the experience of going into hypnosis directly to your client.

In the example that follows, the words in italics are emphasised in some way. An effective way of doing this is discussed in the next chapter.

> H(ypnotist): "I would like to take some time to tell you about the experience of going into hypnosis, by describing how my friend John did this."
>
> C(lient): "Okay."
>
> H: "So, John was curious about hypnosis and he asked me to help him experience what it feels like when you *go into trance*.
>
> "And I said to him that the first step is to [wait until client is about to inhale] take a deep breath and [wait for exhalation] *relax*.
>
> "And then I said, just *notice your breathing* and become aware of how you *relax more with every breath.* It's a natural and easy

thing to do, so I reassured John that *you can do this effortlessly*."

[Hypnotist slows down their voice.]

"John noticed that *your shoulders relax* as you *get comfortable*. And the *tension begins to leave your body* as you *relax*. And your *breathing starts to change*.

"As he began to *notice the spreading relaxation*, I invited him to *pay attention to your eyelids* [client's eyes had begun to blink more rapidly], and simply *wonder what that means*.

"And I said it is as though you *go inside*, to where it is peaceful and calm. You *go inside* to enjoy that sensation and *take some time for yourself*."

[Client closes their eyes.]

"And as you begin to drift off, your eyes can close as you enjoy this experience and float off to your place of bliss, following that feeling of calm and peaceful relaxation..."

At first read, this can seem incredibly simple and therefore more than a little unrealistic. However, it is helped by a deceptively simple technique explained in the next chapter.

EXERCISE

Once again, describe to someone how you lead someone else in to hypnosis. Notice how different it feels if you do so with the intention of leading them in to trance.

You do not even need to be explicit about this, or intentionally change anything that you are doing.

Simply having the positive intention of hypnotising them and giving them the gift of being present with them is a powerful experience.

GRAHAM OLD

62

Insertive Eye-Contact

Analogue Marking is an NLP term which refers to using a verbal or non-verbal cue to mark out words in a sentence. When this is practised in the form of "embedded commands" it is often simply a case of changing your tone of voice or tempo as certain words are picked out.

Within the world of NLP, analogue marking has something of a magical reputation, as examples provided by trainers often make the technique appear irresistible and undetectable. Examples abound such as, "I saw a *scratch* on what I think was *your* car. Who *knows*?" This is supposed to lead someone to scratch their nose. Feel free to try it out.

The trouble with the philosophy of analogue marking and embedded commands is appreciating their nature. All the practitioner is doing is disguising a command that will apparently be picked up by the subconscious mind. Yet, we know that the subconscious does not respond to every suggestion that comes its way. It still requires a meaningful reason to act, even if we believe that it is less rational or critical than the conscious mind. So even if the example above manages to bypass the conscious mind, there is no reason that its understanding by the subconscious mind means it will be responded to.

Personally, I find it more meaningful to think of

embedded ideas, rather than embedded commands. So, I am less concerned with making one-off commands. However, if during a conversation, I can drop in various suggestions and ideas related to e.g. relaxation, I can wait and see if these are picked up on by the client.

In the last chapter, the words in italics were singled-out by a technique that Stephen Brooks refers to as "insertive eye-contact." This simply involves looking in a different eye (usually the left eye) when you want to highlight certain words.

Looking at the transcript, you will see that the following words were selected:

go into trance

relax

notice your breathing
relax more with every breath
you can do this effortlessly

your shoulders relax
get comfortable.
tension begins to leave your body
breathing starts to change

notice the spreading relaxation
pay attention to your eyelids
wonder what that means

go inside
go inside
take some time for yourself

Once the client's eyes were closed and they were clearly responding to John's suggestions as their own, the pretence could be stopped. However, as you practice with this, you might find that you prefer to keep highlighting the 'trance' words through your tone of voice or tempo, just to reinforce what the client is experiencing.

I recommend insertive eye-contact as a technique to practice and get familiar with. At first, it will most likely feel extremely unnatural and you may fear that you are being blatantly obvious. However, I have found this to be amongst the most effective means of analogue marking, as we naturally look from eye to eye during a conversation, so there's no reason that this one would be any different.

Practice and see how you get on. If you encounter any difficulties, they may be addressed in the trouble-shooting guide at the end of the book.

EXERCISE

Practice insertive eye-contact whilst using *My Friend John*.

Make use of insertive eye-contact every time you use a word or concept that might be associated with trance or hypnosis.

Obvious examples would include sleep, relax, inside, dream, drift, float, sink, deeper, trance and so on.

If you struggle to use insertive eye-contact at first, simply look in one eye on their inhalation and another eye when they are exhaling.

After you have practised doing this a number times, practice looking in their left eye for every second or third 'trance' word that you use.

Then graduate to using insertive eye-contact every time you use a trance word or concept.

Actively Participating in Hypnosis

We have considered inductions where the client was a passive witness to the hypnosis being described as experienced by somebody else. There are a number of ways for the client to take a more active role. We will consider three such variations in this chapter.

Playing the Part of the Hypnotist

H(ypnotist): "We're going to do something a little bit different here. And I'm going to need your assistance to do it. I want you to imagine that there is someone sat in that chair there and I am going to teach you how to hypnotise them. How does that sound?"

C(lient): "Er, okay."

H: "Bit different to what we usually do, eh?"

C: "Yeah."

H: "Well, what's going to happen is that I am going to give you instructions to pass on to them. And you will then repeat the instructions. Okay?"

C: "Okay."

H: "Great. Well, the first thing to do is to tell them to make themselves comfortable in that chair."

C: [Turning to the empty chair...] Get comfortable in the chair."

H: "And take in a nice deep breath, like this..." [Hypnotist takes a deep breath and then exhales slowly.]

C: "And take in a nice deep breath, like this..." [takes a deep breath and then exhales slowly.]

H: "And continue to breathe in and out, nice and calmly."

C: "And continue to breathe in and out, nice and calmly."

H: "Allowing the relaxation to build and spread in your body as you do so."

C: "And you can allow the relaxation to build and spread in your body as you keep breathing."

H: "And just notice any areas in your body that are more relaxed than elsewhere."

MY FRIEND JOHN

C: "Notice any areas in your body that are more relaxed than elsewhere."

[Client shifts their position in their seat.]

H: "Then tell them that any time they want to get even more comfortable, they can move around in their chair."

C: "Any time you want to get more comfortable, you can move around in that chair."

H: "What I would like you to notice now, is the changes to your breathing."

C: "Now I would like you to notice the changes in your breathing."

H: "As you breathe calmly and steadily."

C: "As you breathe calmly and steadily."

H: "Becoming more and more relaxed..."

C: "Becoming more and more relaxed..."

H: "With every breath you take."

C: "With every breath you take."

[The hypnotist notices that the client is firmly focused on the empty chair.]

H: "And now I would like you to *rest your eyes* at a spot on the wall in front of you."

C: "And now I would like you to rest your eyes at a spot on the wall in front of you."

H: "And, sometimes, your focus will drift slightly and when that happens you can just gently redirect your focus back to that spot on the wall that you're looking at now."

C: "And, sometimes, your focus might drift slightly and when that happens you can gently redirect your focus back on that spot on the wall you're looking at now."

H: "Your eyes may grow tired and that is fine. Just keep them open for as long as you can..."

C: "Your eyes may grow tired and that's fine. Just keep them open for as long as you can."

H: "You may experience a narrowing of your focus, a kind of tunnel-vision... that's perfectly natural and just serves to remind you to *keep your eyes resting over there*."

C: "And you may notice a kind of tunnel-vision... that's just serves to remind you to keep your eyes resting over there."

H: "So, just continue to breathe in that nice and easy way..."

C: "Just continue to breathe in that nice and easy way..."

H: "And as you continue to relax in that way, you can let all of your facial muscles relax nice and gently..."

C: "And as you continue to relax in that way, you can let all of your facial muscles relax nice and gently..."

H: "Relaxing from the top of your head. Tension leaving your forehead and your temples. The tiny muscles around your eyes relaxing. Your facial muscles relaxing and flattening..."

C: "Relaxing from the top of your head. Tension leaving your forehead and your temples. The muscles around your eyes relaxing. Your facial muscles relaxing and flattening."

[Client's blink reflex changes]

H: "Your eyes blinking more rapidly as you prepare to go into trance."

C: "Your eyes blinking more rapidly as you prepare to go into trance."

H: [Voice has slowed down significantly] "The muscles in your neck relaxing now, such that you might feel more comfortable if your head gently drops forward or backwards, or simply rests where you are, as you continue to breathe in and out nice and easy...”

C: ”The muscles in your neck relaxing, so that you might feel more comfortable if your head gently drops forwards or backwards, or just rests where it is, as you continue to breathe in and out...”

H: “...your shoulders relaxing now...”

C: “...your shoulders relaxing now...”

H: “...And as you continue to relax further and further...”

C: “...And as you continue to relax further and further...”

H: “drifting deeper and deeper into that experience...”

C: “drifting deeper and deeper into that experience...”

H: “Any time you want to allow that head to rest, and gently close your eyes, you can let your head gently drop forward... going deeper and deeper into that experience... as it continues to spread from the top of your head all the way down to the tip of your toes...”

C: “Any time you want to allow your head to

rest, and gently close your eyes, you can let your head drop forward... going deeper into that experience, as it continues to spread from the top of your head all the way down to the tip of your toes..."

H: "You can let those eyes just close whenever you like... resting comfortably..."

C: "You can let those eyes close whenever you like... resting comfortably."

[The client's eyes close...]

Another way to carry out this version is to have the client repeat the instructions in their head. However, they are to look at the empty chair as they do so. Then, when they have given the instructions, they are to look back at you. This has the advantage of you speaking the instructions directly to the client who is waiting patiently to receive them from you.

If you are planning to use this variation, you will want to give some thought to the layout of your room. Otherwise, your client might leave complaining of a sore neck!

Playing the Part of the Hypnotee

A second way for your client to actively participate in the *My Friend John* process is by playing the part of the hypnotee. Of course, in reality, they *are* the hypnotee, but in the induction they mirror the actions of someone else being hypnotised.

H(ypnotist): "Okay, let's do something a little bit different."

C(lient): "Okay."

H: "I'm going to ask you to imagine that I am hypnotising someone over there."

C: "Okay."

H: "And everything I say to them, I want you to imagine them doing it and then act it out – almost giving us a visual clue as to what they would be experiencing. Does that make sense?"

C: "Yes, I think so."

H: "I'll guide you along for the first couple of steps, so you'll be fine."

C: "Okay."

H: "Just so that it's clear when I'm addressing the person over there, I'll call them John. So, John, I'd like you to go ahead now and take a nice deep breath. So, if you imagine John doing that and then show us both what he did, by taking a deep breath..."

C: [Takes deep breath]

H: "And once again, take a nice deep breath."

C: [Takes deep breath]

H: "And John, you may find that your eyes want to close as soon as you begin to feel relaxed, but I'm going to ask you to keep them open for as long as you can, or until I tell you to close them."

C: [Blinks, as continues to breath slowly and calmly]

H: "Now, just pick a spot on the back of your hand that you can look at."

C: [Turns to look at the back of their left hand]

H: "And in a moment, I want you to become aware of the difference in your arms. You will notice that one of your arms feels lighter than the other one, which feels heavy by contrast."

C: [Continues to look at hand]

H: "And when one of your hands feels lighter than the other, you can close your eyes, but continue to focus on that spot on the back of your hand, as if you can see through your eyelids."

C: [Closes eyes]

H: "And whichever hand feels the lightest,

look – through your eyelids – at the back of that hand."

C: [Takes a deep breath]

H: "And all through this process, you can keep on breathing in that relaxing way... taking in peace and calm... letting go of any stress and tension..."

H: "And as that hand feels light, you can be profoundly aware of how heavy the other hand feels in contrast. And as that heavy hand almost pushes down on your lap [speaking on the client's inhalations...] you can become aware of the other hand beginning to feel lighter and lighter, lighter and lighter, beginning to feel incredibly light, as if it is too light to hold down."

H: "And it might start in the fingertips, or it might start at the wrist, but very slowly that arm is going to begin rising up. In its own time, it will feel so light that it just starts to rise up into the air, as if it has twelve bright red helium balloons tied onto it, and your arm floats up with the balloons.

C: [Left arm begins to lift up.]

H: "Lifting up, floating like those balloons, rising higher and higher."

The induction continued until the client's hand was

above their head. The hypnotist then said:

> H: "And when I touch you on the shoulder, your arm can drop down and you can go deeply into a profound state of hypnosis."

He then touched the client's shoulder, thereby ending the *My Friend John* pretence.

Mixing the Two

The third way for the client to actively participate in the process is a combination of the previous two. The hypnotist may begin with instructions like:

> H: "I am going to make suggestions to *My Friend John*, who is sat in that chair there. I would like you to hear the suggestions, process them, then imagine saying them yourself to John and then also imagine how John might experience them.
>
> "So, you will process my instructions on two levels. You will be my assistant hypnotist, by understanding the instructions and passing them on. Yet, you will also be a test client, as you process the instructions and experience them as John would. Does that make sense?"

It may sound convoluted, but it is more straightforward in practice than it sounds. You are simply asking someone to assist you by imagining being the hypnotist and the client at the same time. And you ask them to run your instructions through their mind to process them on both levels.

You can suggest that this is to assist you in understanding how the suggestions are experienced. Or you can be completely upfront and say that this is a really interesting way to go into hypnosis. It is incredibly powerful for the client, as it enables them to hear each suggestion twice.

EXERCISE

Practice the Actively Participating version of Hypnosis.

Ask your client to play the part of the hypnotist.

Ask your client to play the part of the hypnotee.

Ask your client to play both parts.

As you continue to practice – particularly the Mixing the Two variation – see how you get on with *My Friend John* when you are explicit about what you are doing.

GRAHAM OLD

Rolling with Resistance

The *My Friend John* induction is often touted as useful for those clients that might be labelled as "resistant." Although this may be true, as far as it goes, it is useful for us to pause at this point and consider the phenomenon of the so-called resistant client.

In 1984, Steve de Shazer, one of the pioneers of Solution-Focused Brief Therapy, published an important article entitled 'The Death of Resistance.' In the article, de Shazer argues that the concept of resistance is a bad idea and a hindrance to therapists. According to him, what works better is to view therapy as a process of cooperation between therapist and client. Resistance is therefore seen as a unique way of cooperating. De Shazer proposed that everything the client says or does can best be seen as an attempt to help the therapy process move forward. When the client said or did something the therapist did not understand right away, the therapist should not confront the client. Instead, the therapist should assume that the client had a good reason for saying or doing what they did. Approaching the client creatively and constructively in this way is thought to help build cooperation.

Ten years later, de Shazer wrote a follow-up piece entitled, 'Resistance Revisited.' In that article, de Shazer wrote of the evolution that the concept of resistance goes through:

> A funny thing happens to concepts over time. No matter how useful any concept might be at the start, eventually they all seem to become reified. Instead of remaining explanatory metaphors, they become facts. That is, rather than saying "it is as if the client is resisting change," once reified, people begin to say things like "the client is resisting" and eventually they begin to say that "resistance exists and must be sought out." At this point, the concept has outlived its usefulness and needs to be gotten rid of because, once reified, it can never again be a metaphor.

Motivational Interviewing employs the useful idea of "rolling with resistance." Within MI, Rolling with Resistance is a key technique which recognises that simply attacking or confronting someone directly does not always work. In fact, it may do little more than drive people deeper into their shell or lead them to be increasingly defensive or confrontational.

Within a motivational interviewing approach, resistance is conceptualized as the product of an interaction between the therapist and client. It is therefore a description of a dynamic interaction, rather than a standalone characteristic or behaviour.

In a motivational interviewing approach, resistance lends itself to the analogy of water. A therapist encountering resistance from a client is in much the same position as a person in a canoe swept along on white water. Just as the canoeist probably would not choose to turn around to paddle upstream against the current, so the motivational interviewer will not argue with clients, but will respond using that energy to steer the interaction. It is similar to the Aikido concept of blending with an attacker. This approach of sidestepping resistance so that it is not faced directly is crucial in motivational interviewing because direct confrontation is likely to escalate resistance rather than reduce it.

Robert Wubbolding, director of training for the William Glasser Institute and director of the Centre for Reality Therapy also has a positive take on resistance. He writes that, "It is a client's best attempt to meet their needs, especially their need for power or accomplishment."

Clifton Mitchell, a professor and coordinator of the counselling program at East Tennessee State University, wrote, "We tell our clients things like, 'You can't change other people; you can only change yourself.' Then we go into a session trying to change our clients. This is hypocritical." Mitchell, the author of *Effective Techniques for Dealing With Highly Resistant Clients*, adds, "You can't change your clients. You can only change how you interact with your clients and hope that change results."

Mitchell defines resistance as something "created when the method of influence is mismatched with the client's current propensity to accept the manner in which the influence is delivered." This would support the idea that resistance is something that takes place within the interaction of the client and therapist, not a characteristic of specific clients.

Encountering a resistant subject appears to be a common fear of newly qualified hypnotherapists. However, in reality, genuinely resistant clients are a rare thing. After all, someone is paying good money for your time and they do themselves no favours by intentionally resisting what you do.

The rare exception to this may be, for example, smokers who have been pressurised to give up by their partners. Another case might be the rare client who for their own reasons wants to be able to say that they are unfixable. They can roll off the list of therapies they have attempted and how each one has proven insufficient. In that sense, they have demonstrated that they are a uniquely difficult case and beyond help.

However, the reality is that you will encounter such cases far less often than you might think. Yet, saying that you will rarely encounter a resistant client is not the same thing as saying that you are unlikely to encounter or experience resistance in your interactions.

Resistance happens when we expect or push for change when the client is not ready for that change, or is not ready to receive the impetus to change in the way you are delivering it. That unreadiness may be a result of fear, or simply because they do not understand what is taking place. In a hypnotic context, it may be because they do not understand their role in the process. Resistance is not therefore something that exists in a client in a static sense.

When fear is a cause of a resistant response, *My Friend John* proves especially useful. The examples in the chapter *Actively Participating in Hypnosis* demonstrate that we can go as far as asking our clients to respond to our suggestions. However, because they are initially directed at 'John', they feel one step removed and therefore less threatening. This is an interesting phenomenon, but one that experience confirms time and time again.

When we do encounter resistant statements or behaviour, it is easy to fall into a pattern of arguing or to push back. This is a guaranteed way to take the client's resistant behaviour and multiply it by our own resistant response to that behaviour, resulting in an increased experience of resistance and frustration in the interaction.

The less invested that practitioners are in a specific outcome, the less likely they are to encounter resistance. Thus, 'going with the flow' and utilising what our clients bring to the interaction are useful ways to proceed. *My Friend John* is perfectly suited to such an approach as it is not taught as a script to be followed, but a method of working interactively, taking what our clients give us and feeding that back to them.

EXERCISE

Steve de Shazer wrote:

'[R]ather than saying "it is as if the client is resisting change," once reified, people begin to say things like "the client is resisting" and eventually they begin to say that "resistance exists and must be sought out." At this point, the concept has outlived its usefulness and needs to be gotten rid of because, once reified, it can never again be a metaphor.'

What merit, if any, do you find in his approach to resistance?

How might it effect your work with hypnosis clients?

Hypnotising a Couple

The *My Friend John* approach can be used with good effect when working with more than one person. The following transcript documents a time when the author worked with a couple using this induction.

H(ypnotist): "Let's start, if we can, by discussing hypnosis and giving you some idea of what to expect."

Client A: "Okay."

H: "The first thing to say is that by far the majority of people enjoy it. It is a pleasurable, natural and comfortable experience."

Client B: "Cool."

H: [Talking to Client A] "And maybe I can start with you, if that's okay. And to start, I'd simply like to learn about any activities that you enjoy doing, particularly anything that you like to do as a form of escape, something you get fully absorbed in, as it were.

A: "I run. I love to run."

H: "Well, I suppose someone has to!"

A: [Laughs]

H: "And what is it that you enjoy about running?"

A: "It's precisely what you said – the escape. When I'm running, the rest of the world is just left behind and I'm totally in the zone."

H: "The rest of the world is left behind." [turning to client B] "totally in the zone."

A: "Yeah, definitely."

H: "And tell me, what is it you value about being totally in the zone?"

A: "Even though I'm running, it's like the world is on pause, if that makes sense."

H: [turning to client B] "World is on pause."

A: "Yeah. And I don't have a care in the world."

H: "So, the rest of the world is left behind. You're totally in the zone. The world is on pause and you [turning to client B] don't have a care in the world. [turning back to client A] What's that like?"

A: "It's like I'm a child again. Free. Care-free."

H: "Like you're a child again." [turning to client B] "Care-free."

A: [speaking softly] "Yeah."

H: "And what does *that* feel like?"

A: [smiles] "Absolutely wonderful!"

H: "It does feel wonderful, doesn't it? And I wonder where you can feel that wonderful now. Have you noticed it yet?"

A: "Yeah."

H: "What have you noticed?"

A: "I feel at peace."

H: [Looking at Client B] "You feel at peace."

A: "Yeah, calm and relaxed."

H: "You feel at peace. [looking at B] Calm and relaxed.

"And I don't know if you are aware of where in your body [looking at B] you feel calm and relaxed. [looking back to A] Or whether it is intensifying as you [looking at B] continue to relax. [looking back to A] But just notice whatever it is you notice that tells you your body is preparing to go into trance."

"I don't know if you will [looking at B] notice the changes in your breathing [looking back to A] first. Or if you were even aware of the changes there. Perhaps you [looking at B] notice that you're blinking more [looking back to A] or maybe you only become aware of that when I draw your focus to it.

"Either way, it is wonderful that you know how to [looking at B] go into trance [looking back to A] without even being told. Your breathing slowing down, [looking at B] eyes blinking more rapidly now [looking back to A] that calm and relaxed feeling... at peace... absolutely wonderful."

[Client B closes his eyes. The hypnotist continues to talk to Client A, whilst pointing at Client B to draw their attention to them.]

H: "And what's especially interesting to me is that you both possess this ability to go into trance so naturally. Seeing and experiencing it happening before your eyes.

"Like a child again... Care-free... the world on pause...

"And you can enjoy that experience as fully as you are able to, whenever you are ready..."

[Client A closes their eyes.]

H: "And as you both escape into that experience, breathing calm and steady, enjoying your mind's natural ability to take you to such a relaxing place...

"...You can continue to relax further and further, drifting deeper and deeper into that experience, allowing that to spread and enjoying the realisation that you had this ability all along, to relax deeply and rapidly in your own way..."

"And the deeper you go, the better you feel. And the better you feel, the deeper you go..."

If you have never encountered something like this before, it might sound implausible or something only the most elite hypnotists could hope to achieve. However, in reality, it is no more difficult than insertive eye-contact. You simply look at the person to the left, instead of the left eye!

It is perfectly acceptable, whilst getting used to this procedure, to only go part of the way with it. You might simply pause half way through and turn to Client B and say, with a smile, something like, "You look like you're about to go into hypnosis!" This will usually elicit a nod or a laugh. You can then give all of your attention back to A until they are 'under', knowing that when you return to client B, they will already be well and truly primed.

EXERCISE

Practice hypnotising a couple. If it helps, on your first practice, you can be up-front about what you are doing and present it as an exercise for the three of you to learn from.

When you are fluent in this technique, you will find that it feels very similar to insertive eye-contact, despite initially appearing to be more difficult.

Finding Your Trance Voice

In our discussion of analogue marking, I stated that some people highlight certain words by changing their tone of voice when saying them. The reality is that this is usually perfectly obvious to the listener and does not often achieve the desired effect. However, many people continue to practice their "trance voice" in the hope that they will eventually discover that magical sweet spot where their spoken word automatically bypasses the conscious mind and commands the subconscious.

A similar idea of the trance voice is held in hypnosis circles, even amongst those not interested in analogue marking or embedded commands. It is the idea that a certain tone or tempo is somehow inherently hypnotic and will cause listeners to instantly fall under your spell. Such ideas are best left for the history books, under the category of *Myths and Fallacies*.

However, that is not to say that there is no benefit in learning to use your voice in different ways at different times. With the *My Friend John* induction, it is only natural that your voice would be slightly different when speaking to 'John' than when you are speaking to your client. Then when you later speak to your client in the voice reserved for John, it has a certain hypnotic association with it.

Similarly, it is only natural that as you progress in the induction your voice may become quieter and you might speak more slowly. This is similar to when you are lulling a baby to sleep. If you want someone to feel relaxed and calm, it would be counter-productive for your voice to be loud and animated, so you slow it down to match your client's experience. In that sense, your voice serves to affirm what you are saying.

One of the most helpful tips I was given when I was first training in hypnosis was to speak on the client's exhalation. (This is not the case if you are going for an arm levitation, in which case you would want to speak on their inhalations.) I found that it was not as effective to speak on the exhalations from the beginning. Instead, I would do so increasingly as the induction progressed. This was a particularly useful tip for me, as I had a tendency to speak too quickly. This served to naturally slow me down. It also ensured that I was in sync with my clients as my speech calmed down in time with their experience of increased relaxation.

The voice you use to address John can be thought of as part of the process of hypnotic conditioning. Although it is a myth that using a hypnotic voice would send anyone and everyone into trance, something similar is possible on a one-to-one level. If you always used the same voice with someone just as they were going into hypnosis, then you could condition them to associate that voice with going 'under.' In that sense, for that individual, it is true that you could develop a hypnotic voice that would serve to be trance-inducing to them. However, for the purposes of the *My Friend John* induction, it is enough to be aware of using a slightly different voice as you address John. Then, when you later address your client with that voice, they will have learned to associate it with going into hypnosis.

EXERCISE

Practice using your trance voice to signal when you are talking to John and when you are talking to your client.

Gradually develop using your voice with specific clients to signal to them when you are speaking to their conscious mind and when you are speaking to their subconscious.

Eventually, when using *My Friend John*, you may end up with three different voices. There will be your voice when speaking directly to your client. There will be a second voice when you are speaking to John. And then there will be a third voice when you are using "embedded commands." This may sound difficult to monitor. However, in practice you will discover that most of the time you are speaking to John it is an embedded idea. Therefore, there will be little difference between your second and third voices.

The Fake Induction

The Fake Induction is a variation of a 1-2-1 *My Friend John*. It discusses the idea and process of going into hypnosis in order to hypnotise someone.

H: "You've never been hypnotised. Is that right?"

C: "Yes"

H: "Am I right in thinking you're fairly sceptical about hypnosis?"

C: "Yes."

H: "But you're happy to go along with a few things here, aren't you?"

C: "Yeah"

H: "That's good.

"Okay, what I'd like you to do is simply take a deep breath, in and out. Again, take a deep breath... (wait for out-breath, or full in-take) and relax.

"That's okay, isn't it?"

C: "Yes"

H: "And, you know, in reality hypnosis is little more than breathing and relaxing. So, you're half way there!"

[Said jokingly, and subject smiles accordingly]

H: "Well, it sometimes involves imagination as well, so let's start firing that up.

"Can you think of an occasion in the past when your mind has been totally absorbed in one thing, or has even drifted off and been totally absorbed in absolutely nothing?"

C: "Yeah, everyday at work!" (Laughs)

H: "That's good. What does that feel like?"

C: "It just feels incredibly boring. Like I want to bang my head against the wall."

H: "Okay, so that's why your mind drifts off... to escape. And believe it or not, the experience of your mind entering that kind of day-dream state, is what we in hypnotic circles call 'trance'."

C: "Okay."

H: "And we probably enter a trance state of

some kind a number of times throughout the day. We can be sitting listening to a Seminar and our mind begins to drift off. Or, we can be watching a film and get so engrossed in the plot, that we're willing to suspend aspects of reality for a few minutes, as we enter the world of the film and lose ourselves in the story. You might have driven somewhere, on a route you know well, and after a while, you can find your conscious mind drifting off. You go into a daydream like state. You've had that, haven't you, when you get home, or you reach a certain landmark on the way and you think, "how did I get here?" And it's interesting, because it's as if your subconscious mind takes over, whilst your conscious mind floats off into it's own little world, and you go into trance."

[Subject nods]

H: "Good. I'm not surprised to hear that you have that experience. And I'm sure you'll have it again, aren't you?" [Said whilst nodding.]

H: "Yes, because as I said, it's a very common and completely natural experience to go into trance.

"I bet that as you sit there listening to me go on and on about hypnosis here, you're probably getting ready to go off into a trance now, aren't you?! [Said jokingly. Subject laughs and says, "Yeah, nearly."]

H: "Good.

"In that case, what I'd like you to do is take another deep breath, in and... (wait for out-breath) out. And just do that a few more times. In... and out. And as you keep doing that, what you'll find is that it's actually relaxing you more than last time you did it. And, you know, with every breath you take, you become more and more relaxed, for the simple reason that you are getting more oxygen to your brain.

"Now, I wonder if you could pretend to be a good hypnotic subject, for me?"

C: "Okay."

H: "Good. I'd like you to pretend to be in a trance for me right now?

"It could be when you're drifing off at work, when you're absorbed in a film, maybe gazing almost hypnotically into a log-fire, or looking out to sea, or entranced by fish..."

C: "Okay."

H: "So, what would your body posture be like if you're a good hypnotic subject, in hypnosis?"

C: "I guess, relaxed? Kinda slumped."

H: "Good. Okay, so just sit how you would sit if you were to... (wait for out-breath) go into trance... (wait for out-breath) right now."

[Subject shifts around a bit and slides down the chair a little.]

H: "That's good

"The interesting thing... is that even in pretending, you're becoming a little deeper relaxed, aren't you?"

[Subject nods]

H: "You've obviously got a great imagination. So, imagine that you were just sinking, drifting... (wait for out-breath) deeper into trance... That's it... (wait for out-breath) right now. What would your face look like? Imagine how you would feel and how relaxed that would look when you're deep in trance."

[Subject closes eyes and takes a long, deep sigh]

H: "That's good. And your eyes are already closed, because you're a good hypnotic subject, so that's how ready your mind is to slip into trance whilst you relax. And you might want to take another deep breath... and out. That's it. And you can do that a few more times, in and...out, becoming more... relax with each breath.

"You can actually do one better than pretending you're in trance, you can actually experience what it would feel like if you were to really go into trance. Now. Good actors use a technique called "method acting" which means that they pretend to become a character from the inside out, they begin to think and feel and act as if they were that person. It's almost as if they are absorbed in that experience. So let's try a little method acting now. Can you just ... (wait for out-breath) slow your thoughts ... (wait for out-breath) right down, until they just drift and float by calmly and serenely?"

[Pause]

H: "Now, feel the comfort that that brings. Allow that just to ... (wait for out-breath) sink in, to the point where no one could tell that you're pretending... they wouldn't know you were using your imagination... they would simply see you feeling the deep relaxation and experiencing what it feels like to be in that place. Enjoy the experience of trance all the way deep inside yourself."

[Pause]

H: "That's good. I wonder if you can experience imagining that you are experiencing an even deeper trance now...

Deeper down with each breath... So relaxed... And as you continue to relax and enjoy that sensation, your mind can drift deeper and deeper into trance. And as you drift deeper and deeper into trance, you relax more and more as you sink down into the depths of calm, peace, serene tranquillity.

"And if we were really doing hypnosis here and you were... (wait for out-breath) reeeaally going ... (wait for out-breath) go deep into trance, what you would do now is create in your mind a mental image of a grand staircase; a grand staircase that either curves to the left or curves to the right... It has a grand banister with ornate artwork."[4]

[Pause]

H: "This flight of stairs has ten steps. [Pause] You are at the top of the ten stairs. [Pause]

"I would then say, In a minute, you are going to slowly move, in your mind's eye, from the tenth stair, to the ninth stair... From the ninth stair, to the eighth, all the way down, until eventually you get to the very last step. When you get to the bottom of the staircase, you are going to step off into a giant restful feather bed; a place of complete tranquillity

---

4   This version of the staircase deepener is borrowed from Richard Nongard, *Inductions and Deepeners*, p. 174.

and comfort and peace."

[Pause]

H: "So, moving now from the tenth step, to the ninth stair, relaxing deeper

"From the ninth step... to the eighth ...

"And from the eighth... to the seventh...

"The sensation of relaxation doubling with each step... Allowing your mind to drift... And your body to relax.

"From seven to six...

"Six to five...

"Deeper... and deeper.

"Five to four...

"Doubling the relaxation... as you go further down.

"Three...

"Two...

"One...

"And now, with the next step, you would step off of the stairs into a state of total relaxation,

comfortably resting on a giant feather bed...
Now.

"Then, resting on that comfortable bed, you could begin to dream and take on-board the suggestions I would make, and effectively see your dreams become reality.

"But I don't need to count for you, because this is just an experiment, to experience just how powerful your mind is. And you don't need me to count because with each breath you take, now, your imagination is able to hear me counting inside your head. So, your first breath in [wait for out-breath] and out would be number 1. Your next breath [wait for out-breath] would be number two, and so on. And with each breath you take [wait for out-breath] that's right, you go further down that staircase, towards that comfort at the bottom. With each breath you [wait for out-breath] head towards that place where you see your dreams becoming reality, as you unleash the power of your mind."

[Pause]

H: "Down, deeper and deeper. Each breath, hear that voice in your head, each step, down, deeper and deeper. More relaxed. More at peace. Deeper into trance.

"That's right."

EXERCISE

Practice using the Fake Induction.

Try being explicit about what you are doing. Then, with another practice partner, say that you would like them to help you practice something.

Finally, use the induction with no 'excuse' at all.

GRAHAM OLD

Embedded Ideas

We have already briefly considered the notion of embedded commands. This is the idea, prevalent in NLP circles, of being able to drop commands into a conversation that will be missed by the conscious mind, but picked-up by the subconscious and responded to automatically. Think of them as the verbal equivalent of subliminal advertising.

I am mostly dubious of the claims of NLP trainers regarding their success with analogue marking and embedded commands, particularly in some of the ways they are presented. They tend to over-romanticise the subconscious mind and exaggerate the power of NLP. Although there is no doubt that human beings are suggestible, hence the millions spent each year on advertising, there is no evidence that subliminal advertising ever worked on anyone.

To repeat what I have previously written, I would recommend focussing much more on embedded *ideas*, instead of embedded *commands*. Human beings are no more likely to respond to a command just because it is hidden. They still need a reason to respond and that reason is usually because it is meaningful to them in some way. However, embedded ideas have the benefit of being intrinsically indirect and are offered merely for the client to consider. So, instead of commanding them to relax, they are simply reminded that relaxation is natural and comfortable. And that idea can be expressed via analogue marking, in a metaphor, by a story and/or addressed to 'John'.

Embedded ideas have the potential of being repeated in a number of ways, precisely because they are less direct. If they are detected by the conscious mind, that is not an issue, as they are simply an idea you are sharing. There is not the same sense of potentially being manipulated or controlled.

To give a very basic idea of the difference I envision between embedded commands and embedded ideas, consider for a moment that I wanted someone to scratch their head. An embedded command in the form of analogue marking might proceed as follows:

> "I've got this friend, *scratch* that, had this friend. *Your* typical crazy kid, *head* not quite screwed on right…"

An embedded ideas approach might look more like the following:

> [Scratches head]

> "I've been wearing a cap all day. And you know when your hair gets all matted and your head gets warm. Feel like I need a nice shower and a bucket of shampoo!

> "I used to go to school with this kid who always had bad hair. He was always scratching, you know? Eczema, I think. His

fingers were always in his hair. He reminded me of my dad when he used to polish our school shoes. That was one of dad's Sunday evening jobs. He'd get the newspaper down on the floor in the kitchen and get our shoes and then polish like his life depended on it. I've never seen hands move so fast! Backwards and forwards and side to side, rubbing and brushing, just really going to town on those shoes.

"There was this other kid, who had bad hair, he had long unruly hair, longer than most of the other boys in our class. And he always had headlice, so he was always, you know, attacking his head and we'd sit and watch him and before you know it, we're all there – you can imagine, can't you – we're all there scratching away, like we can feel the little squatters on our own heads…"

The second example is less dogmatic about the outcome. It is not a command that must be obeyed, but an idea to be considered. You will also notice that the specific idea was expressed in a number of different ways, not just by using the idea of scratching. Similarly, in the chapter on insertive eye-contact, the *theme* of trance is expressed in a number of different ways, increasing the likelihood of it being responded to.

EXERCISE

Think of an idea that you would like to offer someone's subconscious mind to consider.

Write out three or four different methods of delivering the same idea (e.g. metaphor, tone of voice, analogy, etc.)

Practice embedding the same idea in a variety of different ways.

The Hypnotist's Experience

The following induction is a variation of the Direct Hypnosis version of *My Friend John*. The difference is that the person that you are describing going into hypnosis is yourself.

This induction is particularly effective if you actually take yourself into trance whilst you describe what you are experiencing. With this version of *My Friend John*, I speak on the exhalation almost from the very beginning.

> H(ypnotist): "What I am going to do for you now is describe how I go into hypnosis. See, I never ask you to do something that I have not done myself.

> "So, I will actually take myself into hypnosis in front of you. And I want you to try and empathise with what I am experiencing. So, as I describe something, see if you can get a hold of what that feels like. I'm going to describe this as if I'm hypnotising someone else, just because that's what I'm used to doing and it will be easier for you to follow that way, but actually I'm hypnotising myself and following my own instructions."

C(lient): "Okay."

H: "So, you start by putting your feet flat on the floor. And maybe just rest your hands in your lap. [Hypnotist does as he has instructed]

"At just become aware of your body settling down… and slowing down…

"As you move around, gently, getting more comfortable in the chair…

"And take that first deep breath of relaxing air. And keep on breathing in that way, taking in refreshing life-giving oxygen… and letting go of all stress and tension… Just letting go.

"Just as your body continues to still and slow down, your mind can begin to calm down too. Thoughts may come and thoughts can go, naturally and easily passing through, like leaves on a river, steadily floating on by.

"Perhaps your mind from time to time becomes aware of sounds around you and that's fine as they merely serve to remind you what a natural everyday process this is for you. And maybe you will at times be aware of physical sensations of your body in that chair, which can serve to encourage you to get as comfortable as you possibly can.

"And you may notice those sensations in your

legs, as they begin to feel heavy and relaxed, as if you are sinking into the chair. Or, perhaps, they feel light as a feather, as if you could just float away with your conscious mind. They may even feel completely normal, as you discover how effortless it is for you to slip in to trance.

"And your hands may begin to feel relaxed, noticing if they are light or heavy, warm or cold, or however you experience that relaxation increasing.

"Your vision may have begun to focus softly, as you experience a type of tunnel vision. Or your eyes begin to feel tired.

"And it may be tempting to close those eyes as soon as you feel comfortable doing so, although you may prefer to keep them open as long as you can, noticing as you blink more quickly and wondering what that means.

"Your conscious mind during this whole process may choose to drift-off as if in a daydream, or simply settle down and relax where it is. Or perhaps a little bit of both, as your body continues to relax and your mind continues to slow down...

"Some people even experience a heightened state of awareness as they go in to hypnosis... simultaneously experiencing their mind becoming more still, yet also taking in more of their experience, picking up on every sight and every sound, whilst your unconscious continues to take you deeper into that inner state of calm resourcefulness.

"As you notice your breathing...

"Those changing sensations elsewhere in your body...

"Becoming aware of the tendency for your eyes to blink slowly, opening more reluctantly each time... allowing them to rest comfortably as you continue to go in to that experience."

[Client's eyes close]

"Your mind now drifting to a place of peace and calm, somewhere like a beach, or a quiet meadow, or simply a relaxing hammock swaying in the garden... as you float off to that place and enjoy the sensations you are experiencing in your body and mind..."

EXERCISE

Practice this version of *My Friend John*.

Take note of the difference it makes if you begin to go in to hypnosis as you are describing it.

GRAHAM OLD

Trouble-Shooting and FAQ

It feels really obvious!

When you first start practising the *My Friend John* induction, you may feel like your intentions are being broadcast in bright neon lights. You might feel like your client will never fall for what you are trying to do. And that is a sign that what you are trying to do – and your reason for doing it – needs some tweaking.

I almost always use *My Friend John* in a clinical setting. So, people have come to see me to get hypnotised. I therefore think of it as being conversational, rather than covert. Of course, it is not initially overt, but it is not as if I would be embarrassed if I was caught out. After all, hypnosis is what they are here for!

An example I often think of is a child who is struggling to relax enough to go to sleep. You might offer to read them a story to help them sleep and no doubt your dulcet tones would have the desired effect. Yet, that is a very different scenario to one where a child does not want to go to sleep and they feel their head dropping from time to time, gradually beginning to suspect that you are attempting to trick them into sleep. If your clients feel like that after experiencing *My Friend John*, then I would suggest that you find a way to frame it that does not imply you are absolutely not doing anything hypnotic.

You will have noticed in a couple of the transcripts that I began by saying something like, "I'd like to try something a bit different today." This was my way of saying that – within the context of a hypnotic encounter (e.g. in my clinic) – we were not going to proceed as usual. However, none of my clients would have objected afterwards that I had tricked them into hypnosis, as that's why they were there.

I still feel manipulative when I use My Friend John

If you still struggle with the idea of using *My Friend John*, presumably because it feels too covert, you can always start with the more obvious examples like The Fake Induction. Alternatively, you might want to use the Mixing the Two variation of the Active Participant version of the induction. This is practically overt, as you set out by asking your client to experience what John would experience.

In fact, if you do use Mixing the Two, there is no reason that you cannot be completely overt and explain that this is how you will be inducing hypnosis. That removes part of the reason for using *My Friend John* in the first place, but at least takes away any sense of manipulation whatsoever.

How can I practice?

One of the most useful aspects of *My Friend John* is that it is completely pain-free to practice. Simply have a conversation with someone about the experience of going into hypnosis. As you may be nervous about being "caught out," you do not have to go too far with the conversation, but you can at least experience what it feels like to talk about these things in such a way. At the very least, you will learn that it is almost effortless to help someone relax, simply by talking about relaxing!

Alternatively, you might practice *My Friend John* during your pre-talk with a client. As you describe what hypnosis is like, it is only natural to explain what it feels like to go in to hypnosis. Do not set yourself the target of fully inducing someone. Instead, simply focus on having some effect on their state of mind through your descriptions.

Problems with The Hypnotist's Experience

The Hypnotist's Experience version of *My Friend John* can cause some problems for some people. It is similar to the Direct Hypnosis version, but also different in significant ways.

The key is that you are not merely describing the experience of going into hypnosis. You actually go into trance yourself. You then describe the experience as it is happening.

It is useful to use ambiguous language, so that you do not lose rapport with your client's experience. So, although you may notice your legs becoming heavy, what you actually say might be, "And you become aware of the sensations in your legs."

What's your Objection to Embedded Commands?

I would not say that we have an objection to embedded commands, as such. After all, even the initial transcript shows us highlighting certain phrases, such as 'notice a narrowing of your focus, a kind of tunnel-vision' and 'slip into trance.'

There are two aspects of embedded commands that we feel merit further conversation, rather than out-right objection or promotion. The first is the version of analogue marking where individual words are highlighted in a sentence to encourage someone to, for example, scratch...their...nose. I feel that this is the least useful application of embedded commands, though it is sometimes taught as a ninja-level covert technique that only the very best will master. When I come across such teaching, I almost always feel compelled to raise my hand, not to scratch my nose, but to suggest that the Emperor has no clothes on.

Secondly, the general power of embedded commands can be exaggerated. Just because your hide a sentence within a paragraph does not guarantee that it will be acted on any more than any other sentence in the paragraph. People will vary on this, depending on their understanding of the subconscious mind, but as implied previously, if suggestions/commands to the subconscious were as automatic as some people believe then subliminal advertising would be more successful.

Actually, advertising provides us with a useful example of the difference between an embedded idea and an embedded command. Think of an advert for a soda drink. It might show a hot sweltering day, with sweat running down people's necks. Linked perfectly to that will be the image of cool water dripping down the side of a cold can. We will then undoubtedly be treated to the sound of the can being opened – tisssssk – and see the relief on someone's face as they drink it, perhaps along with the sound of them swallowing.

They can be effective adverts and even the sound of the drink being opened can be enough to make us think, "Ooh, I could really do with a drink." Add in all of the other elements, and you have the rather unsubtle embedded ideas that *you are thirsty* and *buy this drink now*! However, some variations of embedded commands are presented as if your subconscious mind hears the tisssssk and responds like an automaton - "I MUST BUY THIS DRINK!" I would suggest that at the subconscious level, there may be thoughts like, "I'm thirsty," or "A drink would be really refreshing right now," but there is still no automatic guarantee of any command or suggestion being acted upon.

If this rather long-winded explanation has not defended our preference for embedded ideas, please re-read that chapter. Mostly, this is just a matter of preference and style, along with some questions about the more outlandish claims sometimes made.

I struggle with insertive eye-contact

Everything that we wrote about analogue marking and embedded commands also applies to insertive eye-contact. It is not magic. Simply marking out certain words does not guarantee that they will automatically be picked-up and acted upon.

Yet, what the technique does do is underline certain ideas and if those ideas are repeated they are more likely to stand out.

The key with insertive eye-contact is for it to feel completely natural. In most normal conversations, your eyes would flit between the left and right eye of the person you are talking to, even if they focused primarily on one eye. This technique should therefore feel as if you are having a perfectly normal conversation.

If nothing else, this technique is a useful way of making you aware of when you are using "trance words," so that you can vary the words that you use and develop a natural rhythm with them.

They always catch me out

I tend to describe *My Friend John* as conversational, rather than covert. Personally, I have no desire to practice covert hypnosis on anyone. I always tell my client's that from the minute they enter my office, the hypnosis has begun, so I can ensure they get good value for money. That means there is no 'catching me out,' because I am doing precisely what I am paid to do. I was just doing it in a slightly different way.

This question seems to assume that you will be able to lead your client completely into hypnosis without them at any point registering. Now, although that can take place, at times, it is not the usual response. I would guess that most cases involve the client realising what is happening as they get closer to trance. However, by that point, they are too relaxed or invested in the process to object.

MY FRIEND JOHN

They never go in to hypnosis

Some people will not go all the way in to hypnosis using *My Friend John*. This is usually because they are unclear on their role and are not sure what you want them to be doing. However, this is by no means insurmountable.

In the chapter, Passively Witnessing Hypnosis, the hypnotist used the following line to give the hypnotee permission to go into trance:

> "That's right. And you can go inside with them, allowing yourself to enjoy that experience."

Some client's will require that permission, unless you have previously told them what will take place.

Other people may object to what they feel is a trick being played on them. Or they may not respond for their own reasons. This is not a problem in the slightest. Simply lead them through the induction all the way to the end and then say, "So, let's do that..."

As far as they need to know, you have simply demonstrated how you hypnotised someone and now it is their turn. The lovely thing about such times is that the *My Friend John* will have prepared them and they will experience something of a fractionation as you lead them back in to hypnosis. They are likely to go quite deep in response to whatever induction you choose to use next.

What Next?

There are a few resources to become acquainted with if you wish to carry on growing as a hypnotist.

If you wish to read the paper that started it all, you will want to get your hands on Milton Erickson's *The surprise and My Friend John techniques of hypnosis: Minimal cues and natural field experimentation*, from the American Journal of Clinical Hypnosis, 6, pp. 293-307.

Whilst you are reading journal articles, I would also enthusiastically recommend Steve de Shazer's *The Death of Resistance*, from Family Process, 23, pp. 11–17.

www.howtodoinductions.com

As you would expect, we would recommend our free inductions site as the premier website for learning about inductions.

Our web-site offers transcripts of various inductions, from classics like the Progressive Muscle Relaxation to the Bandler Handshake and others. New inductions are added - and annotated - regularly, but only after they have been assessed as useful and achievable for beginners and experts alike.

www.briefhypnosis.com

Brief Hypnosis run live trainings in Therapeutic Inductions, offering hands-on experience in creating solution-focused inductions on-the-fly. You will learn principles and techniques that are not often taught elsewhere, which will take your confidence, creativity and client-base to completely new levels.

Sign-up for the newsletter at howtodoinductions.com to stay informed.

EXERCISE

Continue to practice the various versions of the *My Friend John* induction taught in this book.

This book can not guarantee that you will master the *My Friend John* induction any more than a DVD on playing the Guitar can secure you a sell-out tour at Wembley Stadium.

Practice. Practice. Practice.

And then practice some more!

Contact us at howtodoinductions.com if you have any questions which we have not yet answered.

Bibliography

Battino, R & South, T. (2005). *Ericksonian Approaches: A Comprehensive Manual.* Carmarthen: Crown House Publishing.

Brooks, S. (1990). *"Training in Indirect Hypnosis"* [DVD], University of East Sussex, British Hypnosis Research.

de Shazer, S. (1984), *The Death of Resistance*. Family Process, 23: 11–17.

de Shazer, S. *Resistance Revisited* in Contemporary Family Therapy (1989) 11: 227.

Erickson, M., Rossi, E., Erickson-Klein, R. and Rossi, K. (2008). *The collected works of Milton H. Erickson*. Phoenix, Ariz.: Milton H. Erickson Foundation.

Erickson, M. H. (1976). *Hypnotic Realities: The Induction of Clinical Hypnosis and Forms of Indirect Suggestion*. New York: Irvington Publishers.

Erickson, M. H. (1964). *The surprise and My Friend John techniques of hypnosis: Minimal cues and natural field experimentation*. American Journal of Clinical Hypnosis, 6, 293-307.

Gilligan, S. G. (1987). *Therapeutic Trances: The Co-Operation Principle In Ericksonian Hypnotherapy.* New York: Routledge.

Ledochowski, I. (2003). *The Deep Trance Training Manual, Volume 1.* New York: Crown House Publishing.

Mitchell, C. (2007) *Effective Techniques for Dealing with Highly Resistant Clients.* Tennessee: Clifton W. Mitchell Publishing.

Nongard, Richard K. (2007) *Inductions and Deepeners: Styles and Approaches for Effective Hypnosis.* Andover, KS: PeachTree Professional Education, Inc.

O'Hanlon, W. and Weiner-Davis, M. (1989). *In Search of Solutions.* New York: Norton.

Old, G. (2014). *Mastering the Leisure Induction.* Milton Keynes: Plastic Spoon.

Old, G. (2016). *Revisiting Hypnosis.* Milton Keynes: Plastic Spoon.

Old, G. (2018). *Therapeutic Inductions.* Milton Keynes: Plastic Spoon.

Overdurf, J & Silverthorn, J. (1995). *Training Trances.* Portland, OR: Metamorphouos.

Strozzi-Heckler, Richard. (1985). *Aikido And The New Warrior.* 1st ed. Berkeley, Calif.: North Atlantic Books.

About the Author

Graham Old is a Solution-focused Hypnotist from the United Kingdom. A Graduate of Spurgeon's College, London and the University of Wales, Graham is a former University Chaplain and Community Pastor and remains an active participant of local peace and justice campaigns. He has experience as a Father's Worker and Assistant Social Worker, as well as working in private clinical practice and running the most popular inductions site on the web.

Graham is a popular conference speaker, writer and trainer, with over two decades experience teaching meditation and self-hypnosis. He is an insightful presence in contemporary hypnosis and the developer of the acclaimed *Therapeutic Inductions* approach.